5

things you need to know about

Social Skills Coaching

Your Guide to Better Communication Skills in the Modern World

Roya Ostovar, PhD & Krista DiVittore, PsyD

5 THINGS YOU NEED TO KNOW ABOUT SOCIAL SKILLS COACHING

All marketing and publishing rights guaranteed to and reserved by:

FUTURE HORIZONS INC.

721 W. Abram Street
Arlington, TX 76013
(800) 489-0727
(817) 277-0727
(817) 277-2270 (fax)
E-mail: info@fhautism.com
www.fhautism.com

ISBN: 9781941765425

Dedication

To my beautiful daughter Savanna who never ceases to amaze me with her endless compassion, love and humanity, incredible wisdom, maturity and thoughtfulness, and extraordinary strength, determination and perseverance in the face of adversity. I am honored to be in your presence and proud to call you my daughter.

— *Roya Ostovar*

To my pillars of strength: My husband, Matthew, for believing in my dreams just as much as I do and chasing them with me no matter where our adventures take us; and my mother, Ruth, for sharing your invaluable wisdom with me and always showing me unconditional love. Both of you inspire me to "go for it" and to be the best version of myself.

— *Krista DiVittore*

And in loving memory of Jennifer Ward Oppenheimer, who began a new journey as this book was going to print. Your recognition and acknowledgment of the importance of this work and unwavering support, validation, and appreciation meant more to me than you will ever know. Thank you.

— *Roya*

Acknowledgments

This guide was developed based on many conversations that we have had with each other and our colleagues explaining what social skills coaching is, who it is for, and why it is beneficial. We are grateful for these conversations that helped us recognize the value in creating a guide that will answer families' and professionals' questions about this service that has helped and will help so many.

This work would not have been possible without the support of our family and friends. Your encouragement carried us through to the finish line for this project. Thank you for valuing what we do, believing in our vision, and being a part of our journey.

We would also like to express our gratitude to Jennifer Gilpin Yacio and Future Horizons for giving us the opportunity to publish this guide to help families. And we'd like to thank our editor Rose Heredia-Bechtel—for taking on this project with us and being patient with our process.

Above all, we would like to thank our clients and their families. We have had the great privilege and pleasure of working with you. You truly inspire us to do better and to remember what is important in life. Thanks to you, our work has become more meaningful than we could have ever imagined.

Contents

Foreword

The wide-spread understanding is that socializing with others generally brings meaning and comfort to our lives. When our social skills are lacking, weak, or underdeveloped, we may not be able to fully engage with and appreciate our relationships with other people. So, how do we teach socializing and interpersonal connection, something intuitive to so many of us? The approaches do not always seem to fit the need.

Most books on social skills training target the very young and school-age children and/or those who struggle significantly in this area and lack any social skills at all. The books are written in a language that is appropriate for these two groups only, often accompanied by simple cartoons, pictures, and drawings and thought or word bubbles, a format that may be experienced as condescending or disrespectful by many. The assignments, examples, and scenarios are also designed to address young children and those with significant social challenges. What I have found incredibly refreshing and different about *5 Things You Need to Know about Social Skills Coaching* is that the content crosses all ages, stages, and abilities from a young school-age child who needs to learn basic greeting to an otherwise successful and highly educated adult who just wants to improve certain targeted social skills.

Social skills groups often target young children and, more recently, teenagers, but what about young adults and adults continuing to struggle with day-to-day social interactions? Psychotherapy often targets the co-occurring issues that influence effective socialization and behavioral therapies are often limited to very basic skills learning. What about the individuals who never developed the skills of interpretation, integration, and inferencing, all critical in any social situation? What about making a connection between a nonverbal and verbal piece of information? There is a need for highly focused, individualized social skills coaching for those who are not receiving the support they need to develop very important skills to keep up with the complexities of social interactions.

This easy-to-read guide provides a helpful overview of social skills coaching for a wide range of people who are entering into this conversation. Written by two psychologists who provide social skills coaching to a wide range of populations, Drs. Ostovar and DiVittore have provided a thoughtful and comprehensive perspective on the importance of developing skills at any time in your life, incorporating wisdom and knowledge from their experience providing coaching and therapy. They share what they have seen benefit so many individuals.

In consulting and working with Dr. Ostovar for more than fifteen years, I have also seen this approach work for individuals with highly complex histories and presentations (including individuals diagnosed with nonverbal learning disorder and autism spectrum disorders), as well as individuals who are considered high-functioning and just need support in a specific set of skills. Because needs vary given the person's developmental level and where the person is in life, the individuality and customizability of social skills coaching provides the necessary level of support to identify what areas need attention.

Among the best features of this book are the practical strategies that can be used within social skills coaching. Although many of us may incorporate these strategies into our life without even being aware of doing so, the way the authors explain their different strategies is relatable and approachable for individuals who may have to work harder at socializing.

Most importantly, the authors emphasize an approach that treats the individual from a supportive and strengths-based approach. Instead of emphasizing what the individual is doing wrong or not doing at all, the authors provide the sense that social skills coaching is meant to work toward the individual's goal by further developing the skills the individual brings to the table. This allows the individual to feel empowered and confident to try socializing in a different way. The authors' description of coaching as similar to coaching in sports demonstrates the idea that the social skills coach is not there only to teach and for practice, but also to encourage self-awareness and reflect on the individual's progress.

This well-written short guide is a wonderful resource for everyone, beginners and experts alike, exploring how to incorporate social skills coaching into their lives and practices. As you will learn throughout the easy-to-follow guide, this innovative approach to understanding and learning social skills coaching fills a gap in the current available resources on the topic.

— **Blaise Aguirre, MD**
Medical Director
3East DBT-Continuum
McLean Hospital
Assistant Professor of Psychiatry
Harvard Medical School

Blaise Aguirre, MD, is an expert in child, adolescent, and adult psychotherapy, including dialectical behavior therapy (DBT) and medication evaluation and management. He is the founding medical director of the 3East Girls Intensive and Step-Down programs, unique, residential DBT programs for young women exhibiting self-endangering behaviors and borderline personality disorder (BPD) traits. Dr. Aguirre has been a staff psychiatrist at McLean Hospital since 2000 and is nationally and internationally recognized for his extensive work in the treatment of mood and personality disorders in adolescents. He lectures regularly in Europe, Africa, and the Middle East on BPD and DBT.

Dr. Aguirre is the author of:

- *Borderline Personality Disorder in Adolescents*
- *Depression (Biographies of Disease)*
- *Mindfulness for Borderline Personality Disorder* (co-author)
- *Helping Your Troubled Teen*

Introduction

We all know the importance and value of coaching for many different skills—singing, acting, playing a sport, and even teaching—but not all of us know there are coaching resources for improving social skills. Most people just admire those who are comfortable in any social situation and can have a conversation about anything and with anyone. We think of these people as just being lucky and having been born with a wonderful, natural gift. But that is only partially true. Social skills, much like any other skill, can be learned and improved. Now, most of us will probably never be as comfortable in front of crowds as a talk show host, but we can all improve our skills and learn ways to manage different social situations more easily and with more confidence.

Social language is much like any other language, and social language skills are like any other skills—they can be learned and improved with practice. If we think about the skills required for any sport, we know right away that the role of the coach is critical. This is true whether we are talking about first-grade soccer or Olympic swimming. The same is true for social skills. The difference is that the idea of being coached on our social skills is new to us and we have to get comfortable with it, just as we do with any new idea.

In our experience, most people take a little time to get used to the idea of having a coach for social skills. The immediate reaction when we suggest social skills coaching is, "What's that? You want to teach me how to talk to people?! I don't need that... I have friends, you know?" But Michael Phelps, the most decorated Olympian of all time with 28 medals, never thought of the idea of having a swim coach as offensive or a sign of weakness. We must think of social coaches in the way we think about athletic coaches.

If we think about what coaches do and how they help, we will feel much more comfortable with the idea of social skills coaching.

Coaches are on your side, no matter what skills you are trying to learn or improve. Coaches help you set your goals and identify areas in which you want to improve. They teach you the skills you need, encourage you to practice what you have learned, fine tune your skills, praise you along the way, encourage you, help you take a different perspective, challenge you, motivate you, help you believe in yourself, increase the likelihood that you will apply your skills, and ultimately help you reach your maximum potential. They are excellent collaborators and work with you to achieve your goals in the way that makes the most sense for you.

Most people can benefit from some degree of social skills coaching, whether it is learning proper greetings, body language and facial expressions, conflict resolution, perspective taking, and saying things more effectively. We know social skills training helps those with autism spectrum disorders, social pragmatics disorder, and non-verbal learning disorder, but any social skill goal can be achieved through social skills coaching.

A social coach is someone with knowledge and experience who understands not only social coaching but also how to teach the skills. Great athletes don't necessarily make the best athletic coaches. Good coaching is far beyond knowing and playing the game. It also involves the ability to guide players and fine tune their skills. With input from the coach, a great basketball player can make a small adjustment to his/her wrist and make even more shots successfully than before. In social skills coaching, a good coach can, with the right input, help someone with small but critical nuances of social relationships, facial expressions, body language, and more. A small adjustment makes a world of difference.

This guide to social skills coaching offers a quick and informative tour of what this fascinating and rather new information is and how it can make a difference in so many people's lives.

What Is Social Skills Coaching?

Social skills coaching is simply coaching someone to help themselves feel more comfortable and successful in different social situations. It is a one-to-one skills-based training that addresses specific challenges an individual has in navigating her or his social environment. This service helps develop an individual's ability to communicate with others more effectively. It is intended to be practical, interactive, functional, and specifically tailored to the individual.

Many individuals explain how they are often caught off-guard, confused, and unsure or surprised in social interactions or after a social interaction. This is because they do not grasp the unspoken expectations, cues, subtleties of the interactions or cannot recognize the boundaries and limits to understand everything they need to. One way a client explained it puts how some individuals are feeling in perspective for us. She recalled Elle from the movie *Legally Blonde* showing up to a normal party in a bunny costume and feeling so embarrassed and surprised that nobody else at this party was in a costume. Can you imagine what that would feel like? In the movie, Elle is being set up and given the wrong information. "I feel like Elle every day of my life," she said. Our client was letting us know every day she feels like she has been given the wrong information about a social interaction, or she is missing some important information which everyone else just somehow naturally seems to get on their own. "It feels like I am always walking in, in the middle of a conversation ... it is so confusing." She misses something, which can cause her to feel left out, embarrassed, and unaware. These are the individuals whose families are always kicking them under the table to stop talking, telling them after the fact that a joke they said wasn't appropriate, or something they did or say was offensive.

For those with social skills challenges, there appears to be great difficulty in social situations with taking in all the verbal and nonverbal information and cues, integrating them, interpreting them quickly and accurately, making inferences based on all the information and experiences, seeing the big picture and acting accordingly.

Additionally, individuals will explain how hard they are working within social interactions to understand what is going on, what they should say, how they should say it, when they should say something, what to do when other people laugh, when is it time to stop joking, etc. It is a lot of work cognitively and emotionally and they may end up feeling drained and exhausted after each social interaction. While for those functioning with ease social interactions feel joyful and rejuvenating, for those with social skills challenges they feel tiring and take a lot out of them. For many of us, little thought goes into having a conversation with others. The skills seem to come naturally and effortlessly. And because of the extensive amount of work they do planning and strategizing, they may miss very important information that is being communicated or miss the appropriate opportunity to communicate what they want to.

Teaching these skills should enable the individual to interact more comfortably with both familiar and unfamiliar people. Think about this training as a way to learn or re-learn verbal and non-verbal language. Just as an academic course or an immersion approach can help you learn a new language such as Italian or Spanish, social skills coaching provides the knowledge and skills to communicate effectively with others by learning and practicing in a variety of settings. The more you practice, the better you will get. Furthermore, with a coach by your side, helping you make the necessary adjustments in real time, you can learn to speak the language comfortably and fluently.

Some of the social communication skills that are taught through such training include:

- Becoming more aware of and understanding non-verbal communication (e.g., learning to be aware of your own and others' body language, gestures, facial expressions)
- Practicing active listening skills and engaging with others
- Learning about conversational skills and social reciprocity, such as initiating a conversation, exiting conversations,

finding common interests, keeping the conversation going, taking turns within a conversation, and making small talk
- Learning different perspective-taking strategies to help relate to others as well as developing emotion recognition
- Practicing problem-solving and conflict resolution skills
- Understanding non-literal language, such as sarcasm, analogies, and metaphors
- Learning about the process of creating, developing, and maintaining friendships and relationships
- Handling rejection and rumors
- Understanding and improving communication via electronics such as texts and social media
- Lowering social anxiety through improved social skills

Social skills coaching is client centered. This means that each individual comes in with a different set of skills and a different set of needs. The social skills coach tailors the meetings to meet the individual's needs. This is critical. Here, the client is a very active participant in the process. Good social skills coaching does not involve a one-size-fits-all approach. Generally, the client-centered approach has been found to be more effective than forcing an individual to fit into a highly structured, manual-led social skills training program (Quinn, Kavale, Mathur, Rutherford, & Forness, 1999). The social skills coach uses a variety of methods to teach skills including didactic instruction (psychoeducation), explicit verbal prompting, behavior modeling, in-vivo or real-life practice of social skills, performance feedback, role-playing, homework assignments, video-modeling, and social stories creation, while drawing explicit attention to important social cues and providing multiple opportunities for rehearsal of skills (Beebe & Risi, 2003; Gresham et al., 2000; Laugeson & Frankel, 2010; Rogers, 2000; White et al., 2010). To enhance learning, social skills coaches also utilize Socratic questioning, which is a systematic line of questioning that guides reasoning and is an interactive, collaborative, and non-confrontational method to engage the individual in the process (Laugeson & Park, 2014).

As you may find, the collaborative approach applied in social skills coaching really allows the individual to obtain a full understanding of the skills taught and why they should learn them, all while increasing their confidence to apply the skills they learn on a daily basis and in novel situations. Social motivation may be a necessary (if not sufficient) condition for engagement in successful social behavior.

Furthermore, social skills coaching is to increase the quality of and comfort during interactions through education and practice. The ultimate goal, over time, is for individuals to feel more and more comfortable in different social settings and expand their social circle and opportunities. Many of the interventions are aimed at improving knowledge of discrete skills (e.g., emotion recognition, appropriate social behavior) and concepts (e.g., theory of mind) as well as more complex skills such as accurately processing incoming information and rapidly discriminating subtle emotions in nonverbal behaviors to decide how to interact in a social situation. The following is an example of what a social skills coach may say while watching a video of two people having a conversation:

COACH: People will often use their bodies to tell you if they are interested in the conversation you are having with them. What do you think we are watching for in this video to know if each person is interested?

JON: I don't know, their faces?

COACH: Right! Our faces do reveal a lot of information. What kinds of things are their faces telling us in the video?

What Is Social Skills Coaching?

Social skills coaching is helping someone learn ways to be more comfortable and successful in different social situations. It is a one-on-one skills-based training that addresses specific challenges an individual has in navigating her or his social environment. This service helps develop an individual's ability to more effectively communicate with others. It is meant to be practical, interactive, and functional. Social skills coaching is tailored to the individual.

Who Is a Social Skills Coach?

The social skills coach is a professional trained in social communication and pragmatics. These coaches often are psychologists, counselors, or speech and language pathologists who have a high level of understanding of and ability to assess social communication abilities.

Although many of these trained individuals may also provide therapy services in their practice, social skills coaching is not therapy. This is an important distinction. The social skills coach specifically focuses on skills development by helping the individual learn a new set of skills or improve upon a set of skills he already possesses. Similar to sports or athletic coaches, the social skills coach aims to provide support to the individual and to help the individual build on and fine-tune the skills he already has.

The social skills coach works from a strengths-based approach to achieve mastery of social communication skills as well as to build the individual's confidence in his abilities to use the skills he is learning. The coach works in real-life scenarios, offering explicit verbal cues and in-the-moment feedback, whether the meeting is in a structured setting or in a natural social setting (e.g., library, coffee shop, shopping mall). Furthermore, the social skills coach continually assesses what skills the individual has mastered, what areas need improvement, and which skills need to be developed. The initial and continuous assessment process is imperative to the work and helps the coach individualize the meetings to meet the individual's needs. The process is collaborative and interactive, allowing for goals to be adjusted as many times as needed to meet the needs of the individual receiving coaching.

What Is a Social Skills Coach?

Social skills coaching is not therapy. This is an important distinction. The social skills coach specifically focuses on skills development by helping the individual learn a new set of skills or improve upon a set of skills he already possesses. Similar to sports or athletic coaches, the social skills coach aims to provide support to the individual and to help the individual build on and fine-tune the skills he already has.

Who Is Social Skills Coaching For?

Other people may describe those with weakness in social skills in different ways. They may say, "Something is just a little off," "It's like he got the memo late," "That wasn't really funny, why would she say that?" "He just says anything that comes to his mind," "It's like he has no filter," "She just talks too much, it's like she is talking at you." On the other side, people without fully developed social skills may think to themselves, "Why are people always annoyed with me?" "Why don't I have friends?" "Did I say something wrong?" "I thought he liked me." "What does this text I just got from him even mean?"

5 Things You Need to Know about Social Skills Coaching

We want to emphasize that most people likely benefit from some form of social communication coaching to gain awareness of how they interact with others, how they come across to others, what it is like for others to be around them, and how they may become more effective when interacting with others.

Who Is Social Skills Coaching For?

Most people would likely benefit from some form of social communication coaching to gain awareness of how they interact with others, how they come across to others, what it is like for others to be around them, and how they may become more effective at interacting with others.

Although many social skill coaching groups are typically focused on younger children, social skills coaching can be beneficial for individuals of all ages. As adults, many of us know social etiquette and can pick up on others' social cues to figure out unfamiliar social situations, but some of us struggle to apply the skills appropriately or in different situations. This becomes especially challenging with new and unfamiliar people and settings.

Notably, this type of coaching is most effective when the participant is motivated to have friendships and wants to interact with others. If social motivation is low, the individual will likely not engage in the coaching or practice of the skills being taught, and the teaching material will not have meaning.

Individuals may be struggling in one specific area or in a variety of areas of social understanding that impact their ability to develop and maintain meaningful friendships and relationships. Some of these difficulties may include:

- Inadequate use of eye contact, difficulty interpreting non-verbal social cues (e.g., tone of voice, facial expressions, gestures, gaze, postural positions)
- Problems initiating social interactions, difficulty incorporating verbal social cues, misunderstanding of social rules of conversation (e.g., taking turns, providing enough information to be clear without being verbose, asking relevant follow-up questions)
- Difficulty understanding higher-level verbal exchanges, such as irony, deception, and inference
- Problems maintaining friendships over time, struggling with organizing get-togethers with friends

5 Things You Need to Know about Social Skills Coaching

Consequences of poor social skills may be peer rejection, poor social support, loneliness or isolation, and the development of anxiety and mood disturbances (Bauminger & Kasari, 2000; Chamberlain et al., 2007; Humphrey & Symes, 2010; Rao et al., 2008). Social skills coaching can help many individuals of all ages to increase positive experiences with others to negate some of these undesirable outcomes. After all, most of us are social beings and thrive when we feel supported and understood!

For some people, however, social skills training is an essential and necessary part of a plan to address their significant struggle with social interactions and relationships. Many individuals who have been evaluated and referred to social skills coaching may have received the diagnosis of autism spectrum disorder, social pragmatics (communication) disorder, or nonverbal learning disorder, which is typically diagnosed during childhood. It is important to understand that children will not "outgrow" these social skills challenges. Such problems will persist into adulthood and continue to negatively impact social, academic, and occupational functioning. The Theory of Mind Model (Baron-Cohen, Leslie, & Frith, 1985; Fletcher-Watson, McConnell, Manola, & McConachie, 2014) explains that individuals with these diagnoses have profound difficulty understanding the minds of other people and their emotions, feelings, beliefs, and thoughts. It has been proposed that this particular difficulty may underlie many of the other difficulties experienced by people with autism spectrum disorders or similar issues, including social and communication problems and other challenging behaviors. Additionally, similar individuals often process information differently, which impedes on their ability to demonstrate social reciprocity and spontaneity in social conversations and interactions (APA, 2013).

Given the pervasive and long-term nature of social skills weaknesses, social skills services should be implemented as early as possible to decrease the impact of social skills challenges. While many individuals with varying degrees of social challenges may know social rules and are able to learn social skills, they often have difficulty generalizing and implementing the rules and applying skills they have learned and require additional support to understand the intricacies of social interactions.

Again, keep in mind that social skills challenges range from severe to very mild and subtle; thus, social skills training can help a wide range of individuals. For those with more severe difficulties, coaching might focus on teaching and practicing very basic social communication skills, such as how to properly say hello and introduce yourself. On the other hand, for someone who generally does well socially but finds him/herself in difficult and complicated social situations repeatedly, the focus may be on analyzing these situations closely and identifying a solution. The coach and the individual will then work on strategies and skills that can remedy the problem. For others, coaching may focus on a wide variety and combination of skills. Regardless, such coaching will benefit everyone.

Need to Know:

- Social skills coaching is a supportive, individualized training of specific skills to increase the quality of social interactions

- A good social skills coach can work with an individual to target very specific skills or a broad range of skills

- A social skills coach is highly trained in understanding and assessing communication skills and then to provide the necessary support and education for an individual to learn social skills

- Social skills coaching is suitable for anybody wanting to better understand how to navigate social interactions. Although it may be necessary for some individuals with severe and persistent social challenges, social skills coaching can be modified and useful for most people looking to increase the quality of their social interactions.

Social Skills Are More Than Socializing

A frequent misconception about social skills coaching is that it is helpful only to increase the amount of socializing in your life. While this may be a goal for some individuals, the primary focus of social skills coaching is to increase the quality of the social interactions you have in day-to-day life and to create positive experiences. By having positive experiences within social interactions, you may be more willing to engage in more socializing. Some simple examples of social skills that often result in positive social interactions include smiling, making eye contact, asking and responding to questions, and giving and acknowledging compliments during a social interaction. Some more complicated examples of social skills include those that have to do with the more subtle nuances of communication, such as unspoken expectations, the meaning behind the words, and sensing what you need to do next. Learning social skills will likely lead to a higher level of comfort in socializing more; however, the purpose is to increase the quality of interactions to reap the positive benefits of connecting with others.

 The primary focus of social skills coaching is to increase the quality of the social interactions you have in day-to-day life and to create positive experiences.

Interpersonal Skills

Most individuals who seek social skills coaching services are experiencing some level of ineffectiveness in their ability to relate to others. When you feel like you are able to relate to a peer, colleague, or even an acquaintance, positive interactions are more likely to occur. You also must learn how to relate to others differently. For example, you probably relate to a family member very differently from how you relate to the barista at your local coffee shop or your boss at work. If you are not relating to them differently, it is time to learn that different people in your life require different sets of social skills, whether it is level of formality, sharing of personal information, or other social nuances that are not

always clear. This level of interpersonal skill requires awareness and flexibility with how you present yourself and react to others. Individuals who have difficulty relating to others often appear to struggle in their ability to adjust to their audience's preferences and demands, such as level of eye contact or use of humor. Additionally, individuals frequently have difficulty sharing affective experiences or understanding the perspective of others, two skills that are vital to social reciprocity and the development of relationships (Gutstein & Whitney, 2002). One common strategy that social skills coaches will use is perspective taking, which is often presented as questions throughout a social skills coaching session that help build awareness of how each person influences the social interaction (Laugeson & Park, 2014). The questions are intended to improve social knowledge and assist individuals in reading social cues while understanding the perspectives of others. We have developed an exercise to more concretely and simply demonstrate perspective taking. It is a very powerful strategy that helps portray the importance of perspective-taking. It is called "Do You See What I See?"

Exercise: Do You See What I See?

One exercise that we have developed specifically for perspective taking is termed "Do You See What I See?" Here is how it works:

1. When sitting across from the client, we ask him, "Name three items behind me that you see." He may identify, for example, a lamp, a window, and a bookcase.

2. We will then let the client ask the same question. Of course the answer will be different and may be a door, a clock, and a picture. Both the client and coach are right and see what they say they see. Each is seeing the room from their own perspective, point of view, and position.

3. We then switch chairs and see the room—the situation—from the other person's perspective.

This simple, yet powerful exercise demonstrates in a very real way the importance of putting yourself in someone else's position in order to increase understanding and improving the relationship.

When a foundation of basic communication skills is developed, the social skills coach also assesses the higher-level interpersonal skills, including making inferences, using non-literal language, and practicing social judgment. Individuals without the necessary social skills often misinterpret others' intentions within social interactions and/or make errors in their social judgment, potentially due to lack of practice or inability to interpret information accurately. As you can imagine, this can lead to confusion, miscommunication, and potentially even conflicts because of misunderstandings. These higher-level skills are learned through self-reflection, performing what we have termed Pause and Reverse (P & R) on social interactions, and perspective taking. We will discuss this exercise later in this chapter.

Understanding Nonverbal Communication

A large and important part of communicating effectively with others is recognizing and understanding nonverbal social cues. This includes the social cues individuals should attend to in order to determine if they are accepted into a conversation, if others like the conversation topic, if others are annoyed, if others want to say something, and more. The ability to understand these cues helps us adjust how we react and interact with others. Individuals with social skills weaknesses often lack the ability to develop reciprocal social interactions due to their lack of responsiveness to others' initiations and nonverbal communication. Researchers have also found that individuals with social skills deficits have expressed difficulty comprehending others' facial expressions and understanding the rules of social interaction, sensing the feelings of others, and making adjustments to fit different social contexts or the needs of different listeners (Szatmari et al., 1989; Tantam, 1988; Wing, 1981).

A large part of this difficulty is not being aware of, not understanding, and/or not being able to integrate others' nonverbal cues to make a meaningful interpretation and response. Additionally, the expression of nonverbal communication by individuals with social problems is lacking, including impairments in tone of voice, facial expression, gestures, gaze, and posture (Kerbeshian et al., 1990; Tantam, 1988). The social skills coach provides opportunities to recognize nonverbal communication, interpret nonverbal communication, and use nonverbal communication effectively. By allowing the individual the opportunity to verbally process and interpret what they observe others doing (i.e., nonverbal and verbal social cues) during a social skills coaching session, the individual is also increasing her or his own responsiveness and

accuracy of social perception (Koning et al., 2013). Two exercises that we use to practice interpreting nonverbal communication are called "Put It on Mute" and "Tell Me a Story."

Of course, cultural differences and people's different backgrounds and upbringing introduce different degrees of non-verbal cues in social interaction. For example people of Mediterranean descent are generally thought of as more expressive with their use of facial expressions and hand gestures. On the other hand, those from countries of Asia are generally regarded as being more subtle and of using more restraint in their use of non-verbal cues. In Western countries, people who have mastery of this area of communication tend to grab and hold others' attention. Think of the use of non-verbal cues, facial expression, body language, and hand gestures in conversation as the equivalent of various tools used in writing, such as bold text, underlining, using all caps, highlighting, or changing the font in order to communicate differently with the reader. Nevertheless, it is important to understand and use what is the general cultural norm where you are.

Exercise: Put It on Mute

Another exercise that social skills coaches use with individuals is called "Put It on Mute," which targets reading non-verbal language, including social cues, body language, gestures, and facial expressions. The purpose here is to remove any verbal giveaways. We watch specific chosen videos on mute with the client and discuss what we think the characters are communicating. We practice different nonverbal communication by modeling, mimicking, and/or watching ourselves in a mirror. If a client feels comfortable recording a session, we can then watch the session on mute and discuss the different ways we are communicating with each other.

Exercise: Tell Me a Story

An exercise that we have developed and termed "Tell Me a Story" requires the client to watch a couple or group of people from afar as they interact somewhere, a coffee shop or restaurant for example, and pay as much attention as she can to everyone's non-verbal communication. Since the client can't hear what people who are being observed are saying, she must develop a story about what may be going on based solely on everyone's non-verbal communication.

Self-Awareness

It is also important to be aware of how your presence and interactions affect others, how you come across to other people, and how they experience your words and behavior. A very simple and elementary example of this could be when someone is standing too close to you. In this kind of situation, a social skills coach might narrate for an individual, "When you stand so close to me, I feel like you are in my personal space. Even though you don't mean to, you are making me a little uncomfortable, and this might make other people uncomfortable, too. Let's practice how far away you should stand from somebody when you walk up and start a conversation with them." Then the social skills coach would practice with the individual. On a basic level, the social skills coach is narrating for the individual what he or she is communicating with his or her nonverbal communication and helping the individual develop a "self-checklist" to go through when he is with others. This self-checklist may include the following questions: Am I standing too close to someone? Am I moving too much? How is my eye contact? Being aware of your own nonverbal communication is just as important as understanding others' nonverbal communication.

Being self-aware includes having self-knowledge of your needs in social situations therefore increasing your level of insight. Do you get anxious when you approach others to join their conversation? What do you do when you are anxious? How can you regulate your emotions in the moment? The social skills coach will help the individual recognize any internal feelings that occur that may be affecting his or her communication abilities, then find ways to overcome or manage those feelings so that the individual can interact with others more positively and effectively. For example, a social skills coach may prompt you to take a calm deep breath before entering into a social interaction. These prompts can be added to the self-checklist.

We have developed two incredibly effective and important exercises in order to increase our clients' self awareness and understanding of how others may experience being around them and spending time with them. We have termed these lessons, "What Do Others See?" and "What Do Others Hear?"

Exercise: What Do Others See?

We engage in a variety of activities and exercises with the client in order to help him gain a better sense of what others see when they interact socially with him. "What Do Others See?" is incredibly helpful. In this exercise, we ask the client to video record himself as he engages in a pretend conversation, whether a conversation between the client and the coach or in a role play exercise while watching himself in the mirror. The goal is for the client to become more aware of his own body language, facial expression, hand gestures, and other means of non-verbal communication. Special attention is paid to lack of, reduced, improper, incorrect, or overuse of non-verbal means of communication. With more and more practice, these corrections will become more fluent and natural and feel and look less rehearsed and mechanical.

Exercise: What Do Others Hear?

We developed the exercise "What Do Others Hear" in order to show our clients how others experience hearing them speak. A variety of techniques are used in order to improve how others experience hearing the client's voice. Many clients report that they were told they sound boring or monotone and that they do not adjust the various qualities of their voice to the content of the conversation appropriately. Here we pay attention and improve tone of voice, intonation, prosody, rate of speech, volume, and other related issues. We may ask the client to record herself reading or speaking. She is then asked to listen to herself as well as others in order to gain a better understanding of how others may experience hearing her on the phone, at a social event, or at work during a presentation.

Creating Positive and Meaningful Interactions with Others

Can you think of a time when you walked away from a really good conversation? You might have thought to yourself, "I really enjoyed that conversation," and you probably felt some positive feelings (e.g., happy, acceptance, excited, energetic, optimistic). Awareness and reflection of social interactions and identifying which interactions were positive, neutral, or negative are also social skills incorporated into social skills coaching. When you

cannot understand social cues or are struggling with the basic rules of conversation, it is likely that you don't have many feel-good conversations. This is when misperceptions or misunderstandings of interactions will arise, and the social skills coach will help the individual interpret what happened. Additionally, a social skills coach will introduce social cognition skills, which include expressing emotions, understanding the feelings of others, and empathizing. These higher-level skills allow for an individual to further understand and connect with others in a more meaningful and impactful way. Especially with feedback from the social skills coach, the individual will often be able to notice changes in her behavior and increased effort on her part to interact with others socially.

Many individuals who have social difficulties have likely experienced a lack of opportunities for positive peer interactions, which likely affects the level of their motivation to interact with others. In other words, interacting with others has not been naturally rewarding for them and can sometimes even be a negative experience, so they have learned to withdraw or avoid social interactions. Unfortunately, without the appropriate skill set to navigate complex social situations, individuals without the necessary social skills are more likely to have interactions with others that negatively impact them, including being taken advantage of or being bullied (Carter 2009; Little, 2001; van Roekel et al., 2010). Social skills training is warranted to help prevent unfortunate outcomes like these. By building on mastered skills, teaching new skills, fostering self-awareness, and increasing positive social interactions through practice with immediate feedback from the social skills coach, an individual is likely to increase her social motivation (White, Keonig, & Scahill, 2007).

Exercise: Pause and Rewind (P&R)

We developed P & R in order to emphasize what happens during an interaction by reviewing and analyzing situations closely to understand what difficulties that arose. With our guidance, our clients hit the pause button on a current interaction, an imaginary interaction, or a past interaction, and we process and examine the social interaction step by step. We look at every aspect of the social interaction with the client, asking questions regarding who, what, when, where, and why. With this level of analysis, we can target specific skills to work on and practice.

Need to Know:

Here is a review of 5 specific exercises we have developed and use in social skills coaching to increase the quality of social interactions

- *Do You See What I See?*

  Practice taking other people's perspective

- *Put It on Mute*

  Practice reading nonverbal cues and body language

- *Tell Me a Story*

  Observe others interact and tell a story about what might be happening based only on their non-verbal communication

- *What Do Others See and What Do Others Hear?*

  Increase self-awareness by using videos, mirrors, recordings, etc., to see your own facial expressions and body language and how you sound to others

- *Pause & Rewind (P & R)*

  For better understanding of your social interactions, rewind a conversation step-by-step and remember everything that happened. Ask questions like, "What happened right before?" "What did that facial expression mean?"

"Why did I cross my arms?" "What did they mean when they said that?"

2

Social Skills Coaching Is a Frequent, "High-Dose" Service

Just like with medications, coaching services have an optimum dosage level. In this context of social skills coaching, the dose refers to the number of hours of coaching provided per week and the frequency and length of meetings.

Frequency and Length

For many types of treatment or training, more hours per week lead to better outcomes (Lovaas, 1987, Sheinkopf & Seigel, 1998, Smith et al., 2000). Consider again how social skills coaching resembles coaching for athletes; the more you practice a specific skill, the better you will be at it. Generally, social skills training groups spread 30 hours of instruction over 10 to 12 weeks, which has been found to be insufficient for success (Greshem et al., 2001). Studies with longer-term implementation, meaning weekly sessions for up to 16 weeks, were associated with a greater likelihood of significant treatment gains (Miller, Vernon, Wu, & Russo, 2014).

Research has shown that, for individuals specifically diagnosed with autism spectrum disorder, generally 20 to 25 hours per week of one-on-one services has been found to be most effective (Lovaas, 1987; Maglione et al., 2012; National Research Council, 2000; Smith et al., 2000; Virues-Ortega, 2010). Services can include a variety of treatment providers, such as behavioral therapy in the home, individual psychotherapy, executive functioning coaching, occupational therapy, and other venues in which pragmatics and social skills would be practiced (i.e., at school, social skills groups). All services focus on helping the individual increase his social skills and generalize these skills across settings as well as targeting behaviors, thoughts, and emotions that get in the way of social effectiveness. Changes in communication and social skills may only come about with a certain level of intensity

of targeted intervention or focus (Kasari, Gulsrud, Freeman, Paparella, & Hellemann, 2012).

Ideally, the individual social skills coaching sessions would be provided three times per week for 90 minutes per meeting. We have found this dose to be ideal and a good general guideline in our work. We also adjust it, of course, to fit the specific circumstances of the individual client. This is especially important for those who have never had any social skills training, start when they are older, have a limited time with their coach, and have the attention and motivation to qualify for the immersion model.

The regular frequency of coaching is very important to provide consistent opportunities to learn and practice newly acquired social communication skills. Think of how much an athlete trains to acquire her skill until the task almost becomes an issue of muscle memory. A primary objective for social skills coaching is for the individual to master social skills to a level of "muscle memory," with the ability to generalize newly acquired skills across settings. We want to practice and generalize the skills until the individual no longer has to think consciously about using the skill. In addition to three 90-minute meetings, in some situations, a social skills coach may also be available for coaching by phone to provide in-the-moment support and feedback on an as-needed basis.

> The regular frequency of the coaching is very important to provide consistent opportunities to learn and practice newly acquired social communication skills. Again, think of how much an athlete trains to acquire a skill until it becomes muscle memory.

Additionally, social coaching in the community can be added to or replace one or more of the office setting meetings. This is an incredibly powerful way of practicing the skills learned in the office out in the real world with immediate and real-time feedback and input from the coach. We will talk more about the importance and benefits of social coaching in the community in Chapter 4.

Structure of Meetings

Once an individual's goals are identified, social skills coaching sessions typically include a structured lesson on a specific skill, modeling the skill, practicing the skill, discussion, and performance feedback. It has been helpful to split a 90-minute session

into two halves. The first half of the meeting is devoted to practicing previously learned skills regarding beginning and maintaining spontaneous conversation. The individual comes into the office or other specified location and starts up a conversation with the coach. The coach will help maintain the conversation, often discussing social interactions that occurred since the last meeting. Sometimes the individual comes in having completed a homework assignment from the previous meeting in preparation for the next session. For example, the client may have had to read three news stories each on politics, popular culture, and sports. Perhaps he was asked to come to the next session and carry on a conversation with the coach about these topics in such a way as he would have a conversation with a friend or coworker about current events.

Sometimes clients may think they are "just talking" and not doing work. It is important to know that a good coach is paying attention to everything while engaging in a seemingly casual conversation with the client—this includes skills such as transitioning from one topic to another, tone of voice, body language, facial expressions, hand gestures, ability to gauge the coach's interest in what the client is talking about, the "feel" of the conversation, the ease of keeping the conversation going, whether it feels more like an interview with short questions and answers, and the natural flow of conversation. This is all critical information for the coach to use as part of the ongoing assessment for the client's plan of care.

Don't Worry, We Are Working!

Sometimes clients may think they are "just talking" with their coach and not doing work. It is important to know that a good coach is paying attention to everything while engaging in a seemingly casual conversation with you, gathering critical information for the coach that will to use as part of the ongoing assessment for the client's plan of care.

The second half of the meeting consists of a weekly focus topic or lesson. This is often when didactic instruction takes place, and the social skills coach takes the active role of an educator (Laugeson & Park, 2014). Each week a different topic may be presented, such as conflict resolution or perspective taking. The focus of these lessons is customized to the individual's needs and targets specific social skills deficits. Within these lessons, the social

skills coach breaks down more complex skills into easy-to-understand steps. Depending on the needs of the individual, a variety of strategies will be used during the second half of the meeting to teach and practice skills. Simulated natural circumstances are created to facilitate practice of learned social skills.

> ### Need to Know:
> - Investing time in a social coach will only benefit the individual. Depending on what is being worked on, expect to spend up to 90 minutes 3 times per week with a social skills coach.
> - Meetings will include practicing previously learned strategies and learning new strategies.
> - Coaches may spend time out in the community with clients to practice learned skills in more natural settings out of the office.

3 Social Skills Coaching Is Individualized for Everybody

A key component of effective social skills coaching is the ability of the coach to match the intervention strategy with the type of skill being targeted (Gresham et al., 2001). For example, if an individual lacks the skills necessary to join an interaction with peers, an intervention strategy should be selected that promotes skill acquisition in this area. In contrast, if the individual has the skill to join an activity but regularly fails to do so, a strategy should be selected that enhances the performance of the existing skill. This is where the assessment of social/pragmatic needs comes in.

Assessing for Social/Pragmatic Needs

The social skills coach gathers information from as many sources as possible to understand which skills need support. Family members, other support people, school personnel, and even direct observation of the individual will all be helpful in the assessment process. A social skills coach may interview or have forms completed by these people to gain information. Most helpful, however, is the input of the individual. The social skills coach engages in an in-person interview with the individual to gauge her skill level, what she is interested in working on, and what areas she is already competent in. With all of this information, the social skills coach works collaboratively with the individual to identify skills to be targeted and to form a plan to develop those targeted skills.

If the social skills coach finds additional areas beyond social skills that are inhibiting the individual from being successful within social interactions, he may also provide recommendations for the client to see other providers to address those needs in conjunction with social skills coaching, such as an occupational therapist, psychiatrist, or interpersonal therapist.

Methods Used to Build Social Skills

Typically, social skills coaching will begin with didactic instruction, which is characterized by the social skills coach taking the role as an educator. The coach will directly teach skills to foster awareness and understanding by learning concrete rules and steps of social behavior.

Modeling involves the social skills coach showing the individual what a certain skill looks like. This could be done during a role play, out in the community, or while watching a video demonstration. After the coach is done modeling the skill, the coach will process with the individual what she saw, heard, and want to do the same or differently. This method is often followed by role-playing of similar scenarios with the client. Role playing allows for the individual to think about and practice certain skills that have been taught. The combination of modeling and role playing is particularly helpful in simplifying abstract social skills into more concrete and achievable rules and steps (Cappadocia & Weiss, 2011; Moree & Davis, 2010).

Just as it is important to recognize when a behavior or skill is appropriate to use, the client must also identify when the behavior skill is inappropriate, thus preventing the social faux pas.

The social skills coach may purposefully engage in a role play while omitting the skill to demonstrate inappropriate behavior. For example, a social skills coach may purposefully barge into a conversation or stand too close to the individual to specifically demonstrate inappropriate social behavior. After the role play, the coach will Pause & Rewind with the individual to discuss what he saw, heard, and felt within the interaction and what he might do the same or differently next time. This kind of processing may also be done during a role-play, where the coach will call a time out to help the individual identify what to do next and why. Repeated role playing is a very important part of social skills coaching to solidify the comprehension and understanding of the newly learned skills.

Whenever the social skills coach is working with or observing the individual, the coach will communicate with the individual about how she is doing with the targeted social skills. Researchers have found that performance feedback is most effective when it is presented immediately after implementing a skill and when feedback is provided in a direct, concrete, and specific manner (Anderson & Morris, 2006; White et al., 2010). This feedback can be given during a social interaction or directly after an interaction. The

coach will give feedback on both appropriate and inappropriate social behaviors. If feedback is being given about an inappropriate behavior, the social coach will help the individual remember and practice the social skill to practice in that situation.

Explicit verbal prompting refers to when a social skills coach, throughout the session with the individual, verbalizes and interprets nonverbal and verbal social cues that she observes from the client (Koning et al., 2013). At first, the social skills coach may simply state what she saw and heard, such as, "The tone of her voice lets me know that she does not want to continue talking to me. I should politely end the conversation." As the individual gets better at noticing verbal and nonverbal social cues, the coach may verbally prompt the individual to notice certain things, such as "Did it seem like she wanted to continue talking to me?" followed by, "How could you tell?"

Next, it is time for the individual to practice outside of the office to promote generalization and maintenance of the skills being learned. Homework assignments and coaching sessions in the community are two ways to achieve this. The ability to develop skilled performance of social behavior tends to develop more directly through experience rather than acquisition of knowledge

(Hambrick & Meinz, 2011). Researchers have described home-work assignments as crucial to generalize skills, because independent assignments given encourage application of the core so-cializing techniques outside of the time-limited social coaching sessions and encourages repeated practice, which helps with mas-tery of skills (Frankel et al., 2010; Hudson & Kendall, 2002; Kon-ing et al., 2013). Completion of the assignment is reviewed and discussed during the following session. This review is a critical piece of social skills coaching, as it will help the coach further in-dividualize the type and level of support for the individual needs to master the social skills he is learning. The social skills review can also help customize the session to enact a redo of a social situation as the coach and client go into the community. The next chapter discusses why coaching in the community is imperative for successful social skills acquisition.

Need to Know:

- The social skills coach will always be assessing and collaborating with you about what skills will be learned next to make sure that you have mastered the basics and the higher-level skills—even if it feels like casual conversation!

- Some methods for individualized learning include the following:
  - Didactic instruction
  - Spontaneous conversation with feedback
  - Modeling
  - Role playing and rehearsal
  - Video analysis
  - Performance feedback
  - Explicit verbal prompting
  - Homework assignments
  - Practice in the community

Social Skills Coaching Happens Inside and Outside the Office

S ocial skills coaching that is limited only to the office cannot produce long-lasting improvements in social skills development. Having practice and support outside of a comfortable, controlled, and containing office is essential for generalizing and being flexible with learned skills. A social skills coach will often employ a multi-environmental approach to help the individual develop durable social skills.

The ultimate goal is to increase the client's awareness of social situations through practice in a natural environment, thus enabling them to use the skills they have learned independently and they will be able to successfully navigate their social world. Here, too, the client might feel like she is just out at a coffee shop with her coach and might not realize how is can be helpful. But, again, "don't worry, we are working!" Your coach is observing you and interacting with you in a real-life-situation (in vivo) and is gathering first-hand, real-time, and incredibly invaluable information and data that can't be matched if done any other way. Scientists who study different living organisms will tell us that naturalistic settings provide the most accurate information about any process or living thing they are studying. A person's self-report, while extremely valuable, may not always be the most accurate. Therefore, if at all possible, social coaching in the community should be incorporated into the work.

Social Skills Coaching in the Community

Although it is important for the individual to receive direct instruction from the social skills coach to learn skills and practice learned skills in a safe, controlled, and structured environment

(i.e., an office), it is also crucial for the social skills coach to observe the individual in the community while giving in-the-moment feedback to the individual and providing supportive practice. This is where the skills become more generalized, and this step is key to helping the individual adapt to her social environment. This is also a setting in which the coach can assess what areas the individual still needs more support.

Many therapeutic modalities use the method of incidental teaching, using naturalistic interventions and/or milieu therapy to enhance the durability of social skills with the goal of teaching skills in natural settings, routines, and activities that can lead to improvement of skills (Bellini, Peters, Benner, & Hopf, 2007). Weak outcomes of social skills training can often be traced back to training and intervention that only took place in an office or other decontextualized setting, which leads to poor maintenance and generalization effects (Gresham et al., 2001). For example, for children learning social skills, support provided in a child's classroom setting produced higher maintenance effects and higher generalization effects (Bellini et al., 2007). Researchers have found that using community outings can increase generalization of social skills (MacKay et al., 2007), as these outings provide participants with opportunities to practice their skills in a naturalistic, less predictable setting.

Milieu or community social skills coaching typically includes coaching in everyday environments individualized to the client, encouragement of spontaneous communication, waiting for natural opportunities for teaching or coaching moments, providing prompts for initiation of social interactions, and increasing awareness of how the interaction developed. For a social skills coaching session out in the community, a coach might hold a session with an individual at a coffee shop or a restaurant. The coach might give the individual a task (i.e., hold small talk with the barista) and then observe how the interaction goes. Then the coach gives feedback, does an impromptu Pause and Rewind (P & R) session, or rehearse different ways the conversation could have gone, such as "what if" scenarios. When outside of the office, anything could happen. The coach wants to explore different situations to help the individual generalize skills across situations.

A social skills group can be an option during social skills therapy. Do your research and see if the group has similar individuals with regard to skill level, age, goals, etc. How big is the group? Who is running the social skills group? Due to the nature

of a group versus an individual session, the therapy is typically not individualized; however, such a setting can be a good place to practice the skills learned and to receive more feedback. Individuals with weak social skills can often be too nervous in a group setting or struggle to find a group they are comfortable with. That's okay! One-on-one social skills coaching may be the first step in this process. Often a social skills group can co-occur with the social skills coaching. Talk with your social skills coach and see what he recommends. Remember, skills are more durable and generalized when they are applied in your naturalistic environment, which will mean practice in the community will always be needed.

Social Skills Coaching in the Community

In community social skills coaching, your coach is observing you and interacting with you in a real-life-situation (in vivo) and is gathering first-hand, real-time, and naturally occurring data that can't be gathered any other way.

Social Skills Coaching with Caregivers, Partners, Schools

The social skills coach cannot always be with you in every social interaction, so it is helpful when there are other people in your life supporting your acquisition and mastery of social skills. For children and adolescents, schools and parents can provide social skill support. Depending on their situation, adults may need to be more creative in who they want to help social skill development, including partners or caregivers. Outside supporters can help individuals with behavioral rehearsals in natural settings while providing performance feedback, which is likely to promote better durability of generalized intervention gains (Anderson & Morris, 2006; Hudson & Kendall, 2002; Moree & Thompson, 2010; White et al., 2010).

Such outside support is helpful for individuals to practice and maintain skills outside of the office and without the immediate guidance of the social skills coach. Recently researchers have found that parent involvement in social skills training improves the friendship skills of an adolescent and helps with the longer-term generalization of the skills learned (Laugeson, Frankel, Gantman, Dillon, & Mogil, 2012). Typical parent involvement may include attending social skills training groups, allowing them to know what their children are working on (e.g., education about social skills, instruction of exercises, learning how to give feedback) and helping the adolescent complete social skills homework assignments. Within group sessions, the parent is basically taught to be a proxy social coach for their child (Laugeson & Park, 2014) to increase the likelihood of application of skills at home and in the community. Additionally, inclusion of parents in this way ensures that the skills learned will be practiced and further refined long after the formal coaching sessions end. Researchers have found significant changes to social functioning that were maintained after the conclusion of the social skills interventions when parents were involved with the social skills coaching (Laugeson et al., 2012).

Especially during childhood and adolescence, many parents play an active role in social coaching and facilitating friendships, arranging play dates or accompanying their children on outings. Parents who are either directly involved in the coaching or informed about the skills being targeted may be in a better position to assist their child in the accurate use of these skills outside of the social skills coaching session, thereby leading to widespread, generalized incorporation on outings with friends and play dates (Miller et al., 2014). Research has revealed that parental advocacy and support tends to improve social participation (Liptak et al., 2011). For social skills coaching, a coach may bring a parent to a session, in the office, or in the community to help the parent understand what skills the child is working on and what the parent can do to support the child at home to practice and generalize the skills.

The reality is that not all parents are willing or able to participate in social skills coaching, and sometimes the parents are not available to support an adult child develop her skills. Teachers and other school staff can also be very helpful in an adolescent's learning, development, and maintenance of skills. School staff involvement could vary, including consultations with the social skills coach, involvement in the adolescent's weekly social skills homework assignments, or weekly handouts to share what the adolescent is working on. School personnel should look for opportunities to teach and reinforce social skills as frequently as possible throughout the school day. Additionally, children can engage in play groups, peer buddy sessions, and school classrooms to receive other adults' support and peer feedback. When facilitated

by an adult with social skills development training, peer feedback can be helpful.

For adults, a partner or close friend can help support the adult. It is fairly common for us to receive feedback from our peers, but when an individual struggles with communication, he may not pick up on that feedback. For an adult, a partner or close friend to support the social skills development process can be useful to help identify what he is missing or misinterpreting within social interactions. One important note for those who may be asked to help or who want to help: coaching is not criticizing and is not bringing someone down. It is not meant to be hurtful; rather, it is intended to be helpful and a method of building your loved one up.

> ### Need to Know:
>
> - The social skills coach will likely join the individual out in the community, which leads to generalizability of skills and is a very important part of effective social skills coaching
> - Social skills groups are an option for more practice and feedback

5 Things You Need to Know about Social Skills Coaching

- Parents and caregivers are a great source of support of social skills development at home
- For adults, partners or friends can be helpful in providing feedback and supporting social skill development
- Social skills coaches can consult with appropriate, supportive people in the client's life

Social Skills Coaching Improves Quality of Life

Whence clients struggle with connecting and relating to others, they can experience a vicious cycle often characterized by decreased self-worth, feelings of being stuck, and decreased willingness to try because of the negative encounters they experience. A very important part of social skills coaching is replacing those negative experiences with positive and meaningful experiences to help break away from that vicious cycle, ultimately improving the client's quality of life.

As mentioned before, a social skills coach will make appropriate referrals for a client when the client lacks more than just social skills inhibiting her from engaging in her social world.

Connecting with Others

Typically during adolescence, individuals experience increased self-consciousness and feel a greater desire to be accepted into peer relationships. Adolescents without the necessary social skills may have much more difficulty attaining that acceptance. Often these adolescents are rejected by their peers, bullied, and/ or isolated (Symes & Humphrey, 2010; Tse et al., 2007). They frequently report being lonely, and many are aware of their social inabilities but do not know how to make changes to have positive interactions with others (Tantam, 2003). They can feel stuck.

Research has established that social isolation and loneliness impact physical health and longevity (Cacioppo & Hawkley, 2009; Holt-Lunstad et al., 2010). However, having one or two close friends has been found to be predictive of a more positive outcomes and can buffer the impact of stressful life events, increase self-esteem, increase independence, and decrease depression and anxiety (Buhrmester, 1990; Barnhill, 2007; Howlin, 2000; Jennes-Coussens et al., 2006; Wing, 1983). This is the underlying motivation for good social skills coaches. We must help, as early as possible, in order to increase the likelihood for positive outcomes for our clients.

Not surprisingly, the presence of poor social skills also impacts the development of romantic relationships due to the lack of social skills knowledge to appropriately pursue and engage in romantic relationships (Hellemans et al., 2007; Ousley & Mesibov, 1991). For example, a teenaged male expresses interest in a younger female at his school. Many of his same-aged peers are dating. He starts following the younger female around the school as well as excessively calling and texting her. Although an outsider might view this behavior as stalking, the teenage male might not have the awareness or ability to determine if she is an appropriate potential dating partner or how to approach a female that he would like to date. In this kind of situation, a social skills coach can help the teenage male learn the social etiquette of dating, including who would be an appropriate dating partner, how to ask someone out on a date, how to plan a date, and how to react to the other person's response.

Additionally and because of the inclusion of perspective taking (an important social skill to effectively connect with others), researchers have found that empathy improves after social skills training (Hillier et al., 2007). Empathy is the ability to understand and share the feelings of another person. Without empathy skills, an individual will likely have difficulty relating to others. The social skills coach will use a variety of techniques, including Socratic questioning and perspective-taking methods, to help the individual explore ways to develop these very important empathy skills so he can genuinely create meaningful connections with others.

Anxiety/Depression

When outside of the office, anything can happen. Interactions can be unpredictable, and unfamiliarity with non-preferred topics or unstructured experiences can cause overwhelming anxiety. For example, you may be really interested in and want to talk about a particular TV show with someone you just met, but that person has no interest in talking about that show. If you do not understand social cues, a seemingly positive interaction from your perspective may end up being a very negative experience if the other person just walks away when you are in the middle of telling a story about your favorite TV show. Additionally, most people want to feel accepted and have positive social interactions. People who have experienced repeated negative social interactions due to poor social knowledge likely feel anxious that they will be rejected and would rather avoid social situations than risk rejection or social failure again. This can apply to romantic relationships as well. Researchers have found that individuals with poor social skills report significant concern and worry that their behaviors will be misinterpreted, possibly related to lack of understanding about privacy or social boundaries, and sometimes lack understanding about their own sexual physical responses, such as arousal (Mehzabin & Stokes, 2011). With social skills coaching, some anxiety can be addressed through understanding and experiencing positive social interactions with others through education, practice, and repetition.

Often individuals with social skill deficits know that they have some level of difficulty connecting with others. This feeling of being different from their peers often coincides with feelings of depression, such as self-doubt and low self-esteem (Hedley & Young, 2006). For some individuals, depressive symptoms may be externalized and look like defiance, irritability, or aggressiveness (Ghaziuddin et al., 2002). These feelings typically start emerging and intensifying around developmental transitions, such as from childhood to adolescence and from adolescence to adulthood, when life and social demands are changing. Feeling lonely and not connected with others influences mental health in humans. Adults who lack social skills describe experiencing a profound sense of isolation and related depression, which has been linked to not knowing how to initiate and sustain conversations and relationships (Muller et al., 2008).

Self-Esteem

Poor friendship quality and the inability to connect with others in a meaningful way often take a toll on an individual's self-esteem. Teaching appropriate friendship-building skills and improving quality of interactions will increase the likelihood of developing close friendships and can improve an individual's self-esteem. As the individual learns and practices more with and without the social skills coach, they will start experiencing more positive interactions. With these positive interactions, a sense of "I can do it, I am doing it" often also occurs. It is a similar process to learning how to ride a bike. First a person uses training wheels to develop the basic skills of pedaling and steering. Then the training wheels come off, and another person holds the seat to help the rider develop the more difficult skill of balancing while also pedaling and steering. Lastly, the parent lets go of the seat, and the rider learns confidence in her ability to do it. This last step is also present in the process of social skills coaching after the skills are obtained; a coach helps the client become aware of the positive social interactions they are having with others to show the individual that she has the skills to successfully navigate a variety of social situations.

Occupational/Academic Success

Social skills are critical for attaining academic success, because a large portion of academic success, as an individual progresses through high school and college, often comes with presenting himself well, relating to others, and networking. Demands increase and supports decrease through adolescence and throughout adulthood. Individuals with poor social knowledge and anxiety may lack the self-advocacy skills needed to seek out resources and support (Anckarsater et al., 2006; Soderstrom et al., 2002). Additionally, many individuals may view supports as stigmatizing or assume that services will be unhelpful, and they often prefer not to enroll in special programs as a result (Camarena & Sarigiani, 2009). Social skills coaching can address how to self-advocate to the appropriate individuals and provide education regarding the importance of having supported social skills training to achieve the client's goals.

Deficits in social skills can often lead to difficulties with employment, too. We have known since the early 1990s that social skills are directly related to employment success (Chadsey-Rusch, 1992). The challenges often begin during the interview. Prospective employers may look for some level of social reciprocity in conversation. An individual may not know how to engage in small talk with a potential employer or may dominate a conversation, both of which send red flags to a prospective employer. A social skills coach can help by practicing small talk and teaching the client how to make a good first impression as well as practice potential interview questions so that the individual can have prepared material to talk about during an interview.

Maintaining employment can also be difficult for these individuals, especially if the job requires frequent social interaction with customers and/or coworkers. Core deficits in social knowledge and self-awareness can lead to misperceptions by coworkers or supervisors (Muller et al., 2003; Simone, 2010). Again, individuals with poor social knowledge may dominate conversation, perseverate on topics, make social mistakes, be misunderstood, feel disrespected, become exhausted by social demands, or think small talk is phony (Grandin & Duffy, 2004; Simone, 2010). Additionally, they may unknowingly violate other workers' personal space, which causes discomfort, or demonstrate other odd behaviors such as a pedantic speaking style and poor understanding of nonverbal cues (Higgins et al., 2008). These are all areas that the social skills coach can address through perspective taking, practicing conversational skills, and developing social understanding. Researchers have found that individuals who go through social skills training with some focus on employment success often report more positive attitudes toward gaining employment and a better understanding of the rewards of employment (Hillier, Fish, Cloppert, & Beversdorf, 2007).

Need to Know:

- Missed connections: Individuals often experience loneliness and negative social experiences because of their inadequate social skills.

- Remember that the whole point of social skills coaching is to increase the quality of interactions, decrease missed connections, and increase the quality of social interactions.

- We are social beings! Without meaningful social interactions, we will likely experience depression, anxiety, or other mental health conditions, which often lead to physical health disparities.
  - As social skills increase with practice and support, anxiety and depression could decrease through fulfilling interpersonal relationships.
- Many individuals are aware of their lack of skill in social interactions when they try so hard to no avail. Self-esteem suffers greatly, and the vicious cycle continues.
  - A social skills coach will help the individual see their successes and accomplishments.
- Perceived poor academic and occupational functioning: So much of what we encounter relies heavily on interacting and relating to others. You could be the smartest person in the room but not know how to appropriately express yourself.

- Social skills coaches can step in and teach self-advocacy skills and specific strategies to increase your likelihood of success at school and at work.

How Do I Know Social Skills Coaching Is Working?

You may wonder how you will know if social skills coaching is working for you or your loved one. Although, there is no specific test or tool we have to measure improvements, there is a thoughtful analysis and process that a skilled coach uses. Let's continue with the analogy that social skills coaching is like coaching in sports. When a coach is working with a basketball player and developing their skills, with time and practice there are different sources of information that the coach will use to determine the player's progress and if their coaching method is working.

First, the player will notice within themselves an improvement, such as dribbling the ball for a longer time or knowing they will make a free-throw more frequently. In social skills coaching, our clients notice they feel more comfortable in novel social situations or feel more connected with others. The individual receiving the social skills coaching will notice their improvements. This is one way to know progress is being made.

Second, the basketball player's coach will notice the player's progress at different skill levels. The coach will look at the player's basic skills of dribbling, shooting the ball, and passing, as well as more complex skills of how well the player is using their teammates and being able to read the opponent's tactics. Skill development and mastery rarely happens all at once and takes practice. The coach may have to adjust their strategy or allow time and practice for the individual to learn and demonstrate progress.

As we have discussed throughout this guide, the social skills coach is continually assessing the client's abilities, level of comfort, and progress. For example, we may notice that our client's level of independence and comfort within conversations requires less and less of our cueing and support. Once we notice improvement and if the client has not done it already, an important part of coaching is help client notice their own improvements and recognize the progress they have made. This reflection happens many times in sports and may come out as "Remember when you couldn't even do a lay-up? Now look at you and your hook shots!!" For social skills coaches, we will take the conversational approach of "I am noticing how comfortable you are carrying on conversations and having thoughtful follow-up questions and conversation. What is your take on how you are doing with conversation?" This approach naturally evokes self-reflection and helps client notice progress. We try to do this with small and large progress. This helps encourage the individual, and increases self-confidence in the individual.

Last, in the realm of sports team mates and the audience will notice a difference in the player's abilities. Team mates may be less frustrated and be more willing to have the player on their team. The audience may notice the player taking more calculated risks on the basketball court or being surprised at the player's success rate. In our world of social skills coaching, the individual's support system- parents, spouses, friends and such- can be thought of as the team or audience. We will often hear about our clients at home having conversations with family members they rarely spoke to before, more successful and pleasant con-versations taking place, or finding a friend they regularly com-municate with. For younger individuals who are still in school, we many times get feedback from teachers that the individual is being accepted into a friend group or by their classmates be-cause the individual is trying out their new skills. As you can see, there are three very important sources of information that will let us know how social skills coaching is working: the individual's self-assessment, observation and report, the coach's observations, and feedback from the individual's support system. Rather than using a formal measure or tool that may or may not capture the small and nuanced improvements in an individual's social rep-ertoire, it is more of an ongoing process and discussion with the individual and their support system that will help identify how social skills coaching is working. Most importantly, if you feel like it isn't working, a good social skills coach will be open to hear your concerns, adjust strategies, and work with you to help you advance toward your goals.

Conclusion

For most of us, working with a coach seems a natural step toward developing a variety of skills—actors hire acting coaches, athletes and sports team have coaches for nearly every skill of the sport, and great singers have vocal coaches. So why not hire coaches to better our social skills? Our social skills help us create a community around us and get through the ups and downs of life.

You may have noticed that, at work or in your personal life, it is not always the smartest, most educated, or experienced person who is at the top of their game. More often than not, the man or the woman with the best social skills is the one with the greatest success—he or she can read people well, listen to others and make them feel heard, make everyone feel special, can problem solve well, resolve conflict with great mastery, work themselves easily and seamlessly into a conversation about anything, is likable, is not reactive, and is simply a person others can feel a connection with and is well liked. These skills can all be taught by a good social skills coach to anyone who is motivated and wants to learn. Much like any other skills, the more you practice, the better you will get. The frequency of practice, especially with your coach there, makes all the difference.

We are not all born with all the skills we need. Some things come naturally to some but not to others. We have all seen people who can learn a language, a musical instrument, or a sport so naturally, it seems they were born with the necessary ability. For the rest of us, such skill development it takes effort, motivation, and coaching, but we can learn. The human brain has incredible abilities, and we are just beginning to understand what it is fully capable of. Why not tap into our potential and maximize our opportunities?

In a world that is ever changing, there is one constant. As human beings, we need to communicate with each other. We need to be around others for many, many reasons, including support, learning, and most importantly a sense of belonging. Once you learn and master the right skills for you, you will not only feel comfortable and confident in social situations so that you are not avoiding them, but you will also really enjoy and have fun spending time with others.

> "In a world that is ever changing, there is one constant. As human beings, we need to communicate with each other. We need to be around others for many many reasons, including support, learning, and most importantly for a sense of belonging."

Resources

National Resources:

Autism Speaks
www.autismspeaks.org

The Asperger/Autism Network (AANE)
www.aane.org

SPARK
www.sparkforautism.org

The ARC
www.thearc.org

American Speech-Language-Hearing Association
www.asha.org

Boston and Surrounding Areas Resources:

Aspire: High Cognitive Austim Spectrum Disorder
www.massgeneral.org/children/aspire/overview.aspx

Further Reading:

The Science of Making Friends: Helping Socially Challenged Teens and Young Adults by Elizabeth Laugeson, PsyD

The Ultimate Guide to Sensory Processing Disorder: Easy, Everyday Solutions to Sensory Challenges by Roya Ostovar, PhD

References

American Psychiatric Association. (2013). *Diagnostic and statistical manual of mental disorders (DSM-5®)*. American Psychiatric Pub.

Anckarsater, H., Stahlberg, O., Larson, T., Hakansson, C., Jutblad, S. B., Niklasson, L., & Rastam, M. (2006). The impact of ADHD and autism spectrum disorders on temperament, character, and personality development. *The American Journal of Psychiatry*, 163(7), 1239-1244.

Anderson, S., & Morris, J. (2006). Cognitive behaviour therapy for people with Asperger syndrome. *Behavioural and Cognitive Psychotherapy*, 34(03), 293-303.

Baron-Cohen, S., Leslie, A. M., & Frith, U. (1985). Does the autistic child have a "theory of mind"?. *Cognition*, 21(1), 37-46.

Baron-Cohen, S., & Wheelwright, S. (2003). The friendship questionnaire: An investigation of adults with Asperger's syndrome or high-functioning autism, and normal sex differences. *Journal of Autism and Developmental Disorders*, 33(5), 509-517.

Bauminger, N., & Kasari, C. (2000). Loneliness and friendship in high-functioning children with autism. *Child Development*, 71(2), 447-456.

Beebe, D. W., & Risi, S. (2003). Treatment of adolescents and young adults with high-functioning autism or Asperger syndrome. *Cognitive Therapy with Children and Adolescents: A Casebook for Clinical Practice*, 369-401.

Bellini, S., Peters, J. K., Benner, L., & Hopf, A. (2007). A meta-analysis of school-based social skills interventions for children with autism spectrum disorders. *Remedial and Special Education*, 28(3), 153-162.

Cacioppo, J. T., & Hawkley, L. C. (2009). Perceived social isolation and cognition. *Trends in Cognitive Sciences*, 13(10), 447-454.

Camarena, P. M. & Sarigiani, P. A. (2009). Postsecondary educational aspirations of high-functioning adolescents with autism spectrum disorders and their parents. *Focus on Autism and Other Developmental Disorders*, 41(6), 741-749.

Cappadocia, M. C., & Weiss, J. A. (2011). Review of social skills training groups for youth with Asperger syndrome and high functioning autism. *Research in Autism Spectrum Disorders*, 5(1), 70-78.

Carter, S. (2009). Bullying of students with Asperger syndrome. *Issues in Comprehensive Pediatric Nursing*, 32(3), 145-154.0

Chadsey-Rusch, J. (1992). Toward defining and measuring social skills in employment settings. *American Journal on Mental Retardation*.

Chamberlain, B., Kasari, C., & Rotheram-Fuller, E. (2007). Involvement or isolation? The social networks of children with autism in regular classrooms. *Journal of Autism and Developmental Disorders*, 37(2), 230-242.

Eussen, M. L., Van Gool, A. R., Verheij, F., De Nijs, P. F., Verhulst, F. C., & Greaves-Lord, K. (2012). The association of quality of social relations, symptom severity and intelligence with anxiety in children with autism spectrum disorders. *Autism*, 17(6), 723-735.

Fletcher-Watson, S., McConnell, F., Manola, E., & McConachie, H. (2014). Interventions based on the Theory of Mind cognitive model for autism spectrum disorder (ASD). The Cochrane Library.

Frankel, F., Myatt, R., Sugar, C., Whitham, C., Gorospe, C. M., & Laugeson, E. (2010). A randomized controlled study of parent-assisted children's friendship training with children having autism spectrum disorders. *Journal of Autism and Developmental Disorders*, 40(7), 827-842.

Ghaziuddin, M., Ghaziuddin, N., & Greden, J. (2002). Depression in persons with autism: Implications for research and clinical care. *Journal of Autism and Developmental Disorders*, 32(4), 299-306.

Grandin, T., & Duffy, K. (2004). *Developing Talents: Careers for Individuals with Asperger Syndrome and High Functioning Autism*. Autism Asperger Publishing Company: Shawnee Mission, KS.

Gresham, F. M., Sugai, G., & Horner, R. H. (2001). Interpreting outcomes of social skills training for students with high-incidence disabilities. *Exceptional Children*, 67, 331-345.

References

Gutstein, S. E., & Whitney, T. (2002). Asperger syndrome and the development of social competence. *Focus on Autism and Other Developmental Disabilities*, 17(3), 161-171.

Hambrick, D. Z., & Meinz, E. J. (2011). Limits on the predictive power of domain-specific experience and knowledge in skilled performance. *Current Directions in Psychological Science*, 20(5), 275-279.

Hedley, D., & Young, R. (2006). Social comparison processes and depressive symptoms in children and adolescents with Asperger syndrome. *Autism*, 10(2), 139-153.

Hellemans, H., Colson, K., Verbraeken, C., Vermeiren, R., & Deboutte, D. (2007). Sexual behavior in high-functioning male adolescents and young adults with autism spectrum disorder. *Journal of Autism and Developmental Disorders*, 37(2), 260-269.

Higgins, K. K., Koch, L. C., Boughfman, E. M., & Vierstra, C. (2008). School-to-work transition and Asperger syndrome. *Work*, 31, 291-298.

Hillier, A., Fish, T., Coppert, P., & Beversdorf, D. Q. (2007). Outcomes of a social and vocational skills support group for adolescents and young adults on the autism spectrum. *Focus on Autism and Other Developmental Disabilities*, 22, 107-115.

Holt-Lunstad, J., Smith, T. B., & Layton, J. B. (2010). Social relationships and mortality risk: a meta-analytic review. *PLoS Medicine*, 7(7).

Hudson, J. L., & Kendall, P. C. (2002). Showing you can do it: Homework in therapy for children and adolescents with anxiety disorders. *Journal of Clinical Psychology*, 58(5), 525-534.

Humphrey, N., & Symes, W. (2010). Perceptions of social support and experience of bullying among pupils with autistic spectrum disorders in mainstream secondary schools. *European Journal of Special Needs Education*, 25(1), 77-91.

Kasari, C., Gulsrud, A., Freeman, S., Paparella, T., & Hellemann, G. (2012). Longitudinal follow-up of children with autism receiving targeted interventions on joint attention and play. *Journal of the American Academy of Child & Adolescent Psychiatry*, 51(5), 487-495.

Kerbeshian, J., Burd, L., & Fisher, W. (1990). Asperger's syndrome: to be or not to be?. *The British Journal of Psychiatry*, 156(5), 721-725.

Koning, C., Magill-Evans, J., Volden, J., & Dick, B. (2013). Efficacy of cognitive behavior therapy-based social skills intervention for school-aged boys with autism spectrum disorders. *Research in Autism Spectrum Disorders*, 7(10), 1282-1290.

Laugeson, E. A. & Frankel, F. (2010). Social skills for teenagers with developmental and utism spectrum disorders: The PEERS treatment manual. New York: Routledge.

Laugeson, E. A., Frankel, F., Gantman, A., Dillon, A. R., & Mogil, C. (2012). Evidence-based social skills training for adolescents with autism spectrum disorders: The UCLA PEERS program. *Journal of Autism and Developmental Disorders*, 42(6), 1025-1036.

Laugeson, E. A., & Park, M. N. (2014). Using a CBT approach to teach social skills to adolescents with autism spectrum disorder and other social challenges: the PEERS® method. *Journal of Rational-Emotive & Cognitive-Behavior Therapy*, 32(1), 84-97.

Lerner, M. D., White, S. W., & McPartland, J. C. (2012). Mechanisms of change in psychosocial interventions for autism spectrum disorders.

Liptak, G. S., Kennedy, J. A., & Dosa, N. P. (2011). Social participation in a nationally representative sample of older youth and young adults with autism. *Journal of Developmental and Behavioral Pediatrics*, 32(3), 1-7.

Little, L. (2001). Peer victimization of children with Asperger spectrum disorders., *Journal of the American Academy of Child and Adolescent Psychiatry*, 40(9), 995-996.

Lovaas, O. I. (1987). Behavioral treatment and normal educational and intellectual functioning in young autistic children. *Journal of Consulting and Clinical Psychology*, 55(1), 3.

MacKay, T., Knott, F., & Dunlop, A-W. (2007). Developing social interaction and understanding in individuals with autism spectrum disorder: A groupwork intervention. *Journal of Intellectual and Developmental Disability*, 32(4), 279-290.

References

Maglione, M. A., Gans, D., Das, L., Timbie, J., & Kasari, C. (2012). Nonmedical interventions for children with ASD: Recommended guidelines and further research needs. *Pediatrics*, 130(Supplement 2), S169-S178.

Mehzabin, P., & Stokes, M. A. (2011). Self-assessed sexuality in young adults with high-functioning autism. *Research in Autism Spectrum Disorder*, 5m 614-621.

Miller, A., Vernon, T., Wu, V., & Russo, K. (2014). Social skill group interventions for adolescents with autism spectrum disorders: A systematic review. *Review Journal of Autism and Developmental Disorders*, 1(4), 254-265.

Moree, B. N., & Davis, T. E. (2010). Cognitive-behavioral therapy for anxiety in children diagnosed with autism spectrum disorders: Modification trends. *Research in Autism Spectrum Disorders*, 4(3), 346-354.

Muller, E., Schuler, A., Burton, B. A., & Yates, G. B. (2003). Meeting the vocational support needs of individuals with Asperger syndrome and other autism spectrum disabilities. *Journal of Vocational Rehabilitation*, 18(3), 163-175.

Muller, E., Shuler, A., & Yates, G. B. (2008). Social challenges and supports from the perspective of individuals with Asperger syndrome and other autism spectrum disabilities. *Autism*, 12(2), 173-190.

National Research Council. (2000). How people learn: Brain, mind, experience, and school: Expanded edition. National Academies Press.

Ousley, O. Y., & Mesibov, G. B. (1991). Sexual attitudes and knowledge of high-functioning adolescents and adults with autism. *Journal of Autism and Developmental Disorders*, 21(4), 471-481.

Quinn, M. M., Kavale, K. A., Mathur, S. R., Rutherford Jr., R. B., & Forness, S. R. (1999). A meta-analysis of social skill interventions for students with emotional or behavioral disorders. *Journal of Emotional and Behavioral Disorders*, 7(1), 54-64.

Rao, P. A., Beidel, D. C., & Murray, M. J. (2008). Social skills interventions for children with Asperger's syndrome or high-functioning autism: A review and recommendations. *Journal of Autism and Developmental Disorders*, 38(2), 353-361.

Rogers, S. J. (2000). Interventions that facilitate socialization in children with autism. *Journal of Autism and Developmental Disorders*, 30(5), 399-409.

Sheinkopf, S. J., & Siegel, B. (1998). Home-based behavioral treatment of young children with autism. *Journal of Autism and Developmental Disorders*, 28(1), 15-23.

Simone, R. (2010). *Asperger's on the Job: Must-Have Advice for People with Asperger's or High Functioning Autism and Their Employers, Educators, and Advocates.* Future Horizons: Arlington, TX

Smith, T., Groen, A. D., & Wynn, J. W. (2000). Randomized trial of intensive early intervention for children with pervasive developmental disorder. *American Journal on Mental Retardation*, 105(4), 269-285.

Soderstrom, H., Rastam, M., & Gillberg, C. (2002). Temperament and character in adults with Asperger syndrome. *Autism*, 6(3), 287-297.

Szatmari, P., Bartolucci, G., Bremner, R., Bond, S., & Rich, S. (1989). A follow-up study of high-functioning autistic children. *Journal of Autism and Developmental Disorders*, 19(2), 213-225.

Tantam, D. (1988). Asperger's syndrome. *Journal of Child Psychology and Psychiatry*, 29(3), 245-255.

Tantam, D. (2003). The challenge of adolescents and adults with Asperger syndrome. *Child and Adolescent Psychiatric Clinics of North America*, 12(1), 143-163.

Tse, J., Strulovitch, J., Tagalakis, V., Meng, L., & Fombonne, E. (2007). Social skills training for adolescents with Asperger's syndrome and high-functioning autism. *Journal of Autism and Developmental Disorders*, 37(10), 1960-1968.

van Roekel, E., Scholte, R. H. J., & Didden, R. (2010). Bullying among adolescents with autism spectrum disorders: Prevalence and perception. *Journal of Autism and Developmental Disorders*, 40(1), 63-73.

Virués-Ortega, J. (2010). Applied behavior analytic intervention for autism in early childhood: Meta-analysis, meta-regression and dose–response meta-analysis of multiple outcomes. *Clinical Psychology Review*, 30(4), 387-399.

References

White, S. W., Koenig, K., & Scahill, L. (2010). Group social skills instruction for adolescents with high-functioning autism spectrum disorders. *Focus on Autism and Other Developmental Disabilities*, 25(4), 209-219.

Wing, L. (1981). Asperger's syndrome: a clinical account. *Psychological Medicine*, 11(1), 115-129.

Roya Ostovar, PhD, is an Assistant Professor at Harvard Medical School in the Department of Psychiatry.

She is a Clinical Neuropsychologist and the Director and also the Fellowship and Training Program Director at the Center for Neurodevelopmental Services (CNS), a program serving those with Autism Spectrum Disorders, at McLean Hospital, the largest psychiatric affiliate of Harvard Medical School. Dr. Ostovar has been part of the faculty teaching the Developmental Disabilities (child and adult) courses and rotations in the MGH/McLean psychiatry residency program. She is a Founding Member at the Institute of Coaching, at McLean Hospital.

Dr. Ostovar is an internationally recognized expert in the fields of Autism Spectrum Disorders, Non-Verbal Learning Disorder, Social Pragmatics Disorder, Social Skills Coaching, and Sensory Processing Disorder. She is the acclaimed author of multiple publications including the highly regarded book, *The Ultimate Guide to Sensory Processing Disorder*, which received *Creative Child* Magazine's 2010 Preferred Choice Award in Parenting "Aids-Special Needs-Sensory Processing" category and the *Autism Inventory of Development (AID™)* a critical tool used as part of a comprehensive assessment of Autism Spectrum Disorders and Social Pragmatic (Communication) Disorder, both published by Future Horizons. With her unique lens and expertise in child development and psychiatric disorders, she wrote the chapter "An Overview of Adolescent Development" for *Helping Your Troubled Teen* book.

Dr. Ostovar provides individual and group social skills coaching and coaching in the community through her private practice, Ostovar Psychology, Coaching, and Consultation, located in Belmont, Massachusetts.

More information is available at www.royaostovar.com and www.ostovar-coaching.com.

Dr. Krista DiVittore is an Instructor in the department of psychiatry at Harvard Medical School. She is a staff clinical psychologist at the Center of Neurodevelopmental Services, a program serving those with Autism Spectrum Disorder, at McLean Hospital, the largest psychiatric teaching hospital of Harvard Medical School. In this role she works directly with children, adolescents, and young adults who have neurodevelopmental disorders, sensory processing issues, and co-occurring psychiatric disorders. Dr. DiVittore teaches social/pragmatic skills and skills to tolerate and manage difficult emotions. Dr. DiVittore's previous work has also included working with children and adults who experienced a variety of psychiatric issues, such as anxiety, mood disorders, and psychosis, all of which impact social interactions and daily functioning. She uses various skills-based modalities including Cognitive Behavioral Therapy (CBT), Dialectical Behavior Therapy (DBT) and Acceptance and Commitment Therapy (ACT) to help individuals master skills that allow them to be more effective and fulfilled in their personal and interpersonal lives.